Table of Content

Dedication

"I dedicate this book to the awesome power within you, the devoted success searcher, to create a life a success and excellence."

-Howard Strachan

"Money is a good thing to have, but wisdom is greater. A man without wisdom is like the ocean without the moon."

–Howard Strachan

"Have not I commanded thee? Be strong and of a good courage; be not afraid, neither be thou dismayed: for the lord thy God is with thee whithersoever thou goest."

-Joshua 1:9

Acknowledge

I am over helmed in all humbleness and gratefulness to acknowledge my depth to all those who have helped me to put these ideas, well above the level of simplicity and into something concrete.

I would like to express my special thanks of gratitude to my Rayon Nelson who has encourage me to do this wonderful book on the topic Wisdom and Knowledge of Success, which also helped me in doing a lot of research and I came to know about so many new things. I am really thankful to him.

Any attempt at any level can't be satisfactorily completed without the support and guidance of MY parents.

I would like to thank my parents who helped me a lot in gathering different information, collecting data, and guiding me from time to time in making this book, despite their busy schedules, they gave me different ideas to make this book unique.

The Right Path

Every stage in life operates like a compass that directs us to different

roads. We will not meet at the exact location because of our decisions.

Every decision that we make has significance, even the tiniest choice

that we make reverberates throughout the universe. All of our

experiences modify our lives because of changes. Change is a variable

of life, there are changes that we look forward to and changes that we

fear. However, one thing is for sure, life will not stay the same no

matter how much we would like it to. When life changes occur we have

two choices of how to respond. We can despair that a change has come

and assumed that things will be worse, or we can look at new possibilities optimistically for personal growth and make adjustments to the way we view life.

- ### **The Right Path Quotes**

"Even if your story is messy be the narrator of it." Howard Strachan

"Every great being started by taking one step." Howard Strachan

"One way in finding the truth is to finding it within you first." Howard Strachan

"It's necessary that we get the loser out of our life, if we want to live our dream." Howard Strachan

The Compass of Life

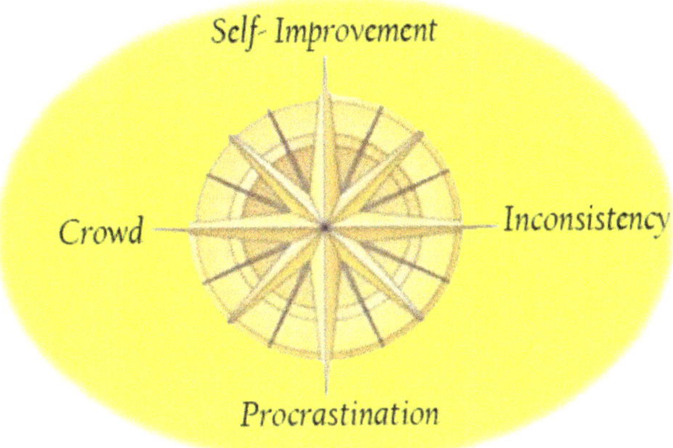

The diagram above illustrates a compass. If this was a typical compass,

north would've been illustrated pointing upwards, east would be

pointing to the right, west would be pointing to the left and south would be pointing downwards, however, this is not a typical compass! As you can see on the northern section of this compass the word north is substituted by the word self-improvement, on the eastern section there's inconsistency, on the western section there's a crowd and where there should be south there's a procrastination. These are the general reference points that attempt to capture our attention and control the needle of our lives, but we possess the power that can exert guidance over the needle.

We must choose to point our decision-making process in the right direction. If we fail to do so, we will be subjected to a miserable life, frittering away our perishable commodities of time, talent, and treasure. When this happens, we lose our opportunities for self-growth, imperishable eternal values that will echo into eternity. We will end life in this world and start living in heaven with nothing.

Put God first in everything you do, put him first when you're failing and succeeding. God is the answer for everything, regardless of appearances. Truth be told, I am an individual with a mental, emotional, and physical countenance of universal life. Constantly improving oneself is essentially to obtain life purpose.

- ## The Compass of Life Quotes

"Whatever life throws at you and it seems difficult, there is always something you can do to succeed at it." - Howard Strachan

"God is the truth and the only way to true success." -Howard Strachan

"Look into the mirror at the man of tomorrow, he alone can modify your path."
- Howard Strachan

The True Essence of Time

All I have earned I have spent, But I don't regret it. In the hearts, I hope my assets have grown manifold wisdom. For what it's worth: it's never too late or, in my case, too early to be whoever you want to be. There's no time limit, stop whenever you want. You can change or stay the same, there are no rules to this thing. We can make the best or the worst of it. I hope you make the best of it. And I hope you see things that startle you. I hope you feel things you never felt before. I hope you meet people with a different point of view. I hope you live a life you're proud of. If you find that you're not, I hope you have the courage to start all over again.

- ## **The True Essence of Time Quotes**

"The greatest challenge and the greatest obstacle you can face is your own doubts."

-Howard Strachan

"We are given 86,400 seconds every day to succeed in life and we often used 21,600 seconds to try to be successful." -Howard Strachan

"One day your life will flash before your eyes, make sure it's worth watching."

-Howard Strachan

Saving Time

The purpose of turning off the lights at night is to save energy. A successful associate of mine likes to say, "It's necessary to succeed in any field." Prosperous people are those who live their lives for a reason. Success comes through purpose, whether it be in sports, business, science, or spiritual growth. People who want to be successful in life start by setting goals. Their sights are trained on an object to which they devote their strength, faith, love, and prayers. They happily give up pleasures that may seem extremely significant to others, to attain their aspirations in life. They will even bear with what others deemed hardship and embarrassment by taking minor steps towards their goals.

A top athlete, for example, "Usain Bolt" did not scruple all his time to pleasurable events such as parties instead he exercises hard to become a champion. A baby's mother whose purpose is to feed, clothe, and educate her child will make incredible sacrifices to attain her goals and many fine scientists have a full record of self-discipline, long hours of study, and research as part of their success story. A successful person wastes little time numbering his sacrifices- his purpose is so great that the cost of attaining his goals hardly seems worthwhile mentioning. A little observation will reveal that failure and frustration also have a common denominator-lack of purpose. An individual who accepts and surrenders to failure is saying that he does not have a purpose big enough to make himself willing to keep trying, praying, and to keep working to overcome obstacles that seem to be in the way of his success. No complications of any kind can long block the path of an individual with a real purpose in life. He will take every difficulty and make them into a successful pattern just to make his purpose worthwhile. Success or failure is not dependent on the number of obstacles, but the sincerity and intensity of one's purpose. Real purpose calls forth wisdom, knowledge, love, and the energy needed for its fulfilment. In regards to Mr. Earlan Bartley who said he has the formula, but if one looks into himself he will see that he has the formula to be successful, through the quality of the purposes which he lives. There are numerous geniuses buried with their aptitude and goals that they didn't bring into motion. This is simply because they have never found a purpose in life that would focus and give directions to their talents and abilities. A life without a purpose is marked by frustration, futility, and disorder that may lead to the feeling that you belong to an abyss. However, it can be filled with activity {finding yourself hobbies}, but activity without momentum is like a boat without a destination, a start without a finish. Persons who don't know where they're going always arrived at the same place whilst, some people try desperately to choose which way to go. To the person who thinks that having a direction isn't important, he is deemed to have no destination in mind. He usually remains in a state of indecisiveness because some events or circumstances come along to bump onto some side alley of his life, where he remains until something else comes along to force

13

him to an intersection. Unless a person has a purpose of his own, then he will try to create another way for someone else.

We are designed for greatness, and happiness, to be successful, and to live a satisfying life. Everyone can set a purpose that is big enough to call forth their hidden talents and abilities. Our talents and abilities are our gifts from God that ought to be used to make life better, but we must decide the purpose in which we invest them.

- ## <u>**Saving Time Quotes**</u>

"Our greatest weakness is giving up. To become successful is to always try one more time."
-Howard Strachan

"Our greatest achievement is not falling, but getting up after being pushed to the ground."
-Howard Strachan

'Choose to focus your time and energy on people who inspire you, support you and help you to get stronger." -Howard Strachan

The Outcome of Faith

When you are going through life's jungle, and you think there is no way out, you're not the first to feel this way. What is success without doubts at times? To have faith is to defy logic, it takes faith to think positively. It takes faith to believe that there is a loving God who cares deeply about our pain. To believe in life, the universe, or yourself after numerous failures is to have courage. Faith is an act of courage. It is a choice to get up in the morning and face our fears and believe that God will help us. To have faith is choosing to believe that even though you may have failed one hundred times there is still a chance of succeeding

once you make an effort to try again.

- ## **<u>The Outcome of Faith Quotes</u>**

"It's never too late to try again; it's never too late to decide that today is the day you're going to succeed in whatever you're doing." – Howard Strachan

"Never give up on your dreams, push ahead, push pass your challenges. Aim to surpass your expectation."- Howard Strachan

"There is blessing in the midst of a storm." – Howard Strachan

What do you think is key?

Try to think optimistically think of what you can do, not what you can't.

Think successful and you will be successful. Be wary of negative influences that can steer you away from your goals.

Our mind is the control tower of our life, whatever, happens in our life starts right here. All of our decisions are there and whatever we are today happens as a result of what we were thinking about all those years. So whatever you think in your heart that's what you are going to be, so if you don't like what's going on around you, you should ask yourself "what am I thinking about", "what do I think of myself and other people", what we think about most is what controls us that is our relationships, our failures in life, our accomplishment all of those are as a result of whatever we think.

. Successful thinking is part of the image of God in man. The universal creative process is individualized and given expression through each person, according to his consciousness of it. The world is a mixture of good and bad, just as a man's concepts and thinking process. The "good" concepts that men have held of the creator as love, justice, and goodwill are showing forth in human attempts to love, understand, and appreciate each other and to work for the universal good.

As I practice accurate thinking, the successful thinking process in me transforms my life. Someday thinking accurately will be a part of the curriculum of every school, college, and workplace because humanity

is gradually awakening to the truth. What we feed into the successful

thinking process in each other is even more important than the

information we input into our computers. Success doesn't start when

understanding the concept, but rather when you fail and pick yourself

up, and take a step forward.

- ## <u>How do you think is key Quotes</u>

"Your optimistic action combined with positive thinking result in success. "
-Howard Strachan

"The best ideas come when you're by yourself."-Howard Strachan

"Very little is needed to make a happy life; it is all within yourself, the way how you think."
-Howard Strachan

"Only I can change the way how I think; no one can do it for me." – Howard Strachan

Building Self with Knowledge

I feel myself becoming distant, further and further every day. The shell I worked so hard to break through surrounds me once again. The blade provides no comfort yet I feel no pain. Will I ever learn to love myself like I did yesterday? Learning is the knowledge acquired through study, experience, or being taught. Experiences make us wiser, learning makes us smarter. All must coincide together with an open mind to ponder and a good heart to wonder about balancing between right and wrong. We gain room for change in processing the increasing progress. With all that often we waste too much on unneeded things.

- ## **<u>Building Self with Knowledge Quotes</u>**

"Most of our irrational responses are based upon our egos." –Howard Strachan

"Self-doubt is the first step in failure, never let one's opinion of you get you down."
–Howard Strachan

"Planting an oak tree is easy, but waiting on it to mature is difficult. The pursuit of the difficult makes us stronger." –Howard Strachan

Continue to Learn

Read, Read!! Read everything that interests you. Take a class or obtain extra training. The first thing that strikes me about education is knowledge gain. Education gives us knowledge of the world around us and changes it into something better. It develops in us a perspective of looking at life. It helps us build opinions and have points of view on things in life. People debate over the subject of whether education is the only thing that gives knowledge. Some say education is the process of gaining information about the surrounding world while knowledge is something very different. They are right. But then again, information cannot be converted into knowledge without education. Education makes us capable of interpreting things, among other things. It is not just about lessons in textbooks. It is about the lessons of life.

 In life, you're going to make mistakes, and it's going to take a toll on you. However, your mistakes are a part of your learning. Your mistakes don't define who you are as a person. It shows the consequences of the real world for the choices you make. Mistakes allow us to apply ourselves more to a situation based on our knowledge from similar past experiences. It has the power to change you into something better than you were before. We use our mistakes (lemons) to make something sweet (lemonade) in life. Life is a journey that leads to greatness, continue to learn new things and also learn from your mistakes, because a collection of mistakes leads to experience.

- ## **Continue to learn Quotes**

"Keep looking up! Learn from the past, and dream about the future. There's nothing like an exquisite sunrise at the beginning of a healthy day." -Howard Strachan

"Learn from yesterday, live for today, and seek tomorrow. The important thing is to never stop learning." -Howard Strachan

"A wise man can learn more from an absurd question than a fool can learn from a wise response." -Howard Strachan

Take a Break from Life's Challenges

Relax, de-stress yourself, the moon is full tonight. The stars are out, faces turned forward. Trials painted end to end. Your heart never felt so bright. As the silence takes over on a late summer night, the riot begins to take place in your mind. The sting of your past collides with the uncertainty of the future with a crash strong enough to mess you up for sure, but keep that chin up, it's not as hopeless as it seems. Don't kill yourself over it. Keep both your wrists clean. If all else fails, take a break and forget. Go get yourself some coffee and pray to God.

"Focus on your destination not your journey." –Howard Strachan

"Success doesn't come easily. It requires an acumen mind to understand it's diversity.'
–Howard Strachan

"Concentrate on your goals and not your audience." –Howard Strachan

"Dear self,
 Don't get upset over things you can't modify or people you can't change. Control only what you have control over." –Howard Strachan

Don't be too Hard on Yourself

Recognize the mistake that you have made in the past and learn from them. We all make mistakes, we all have a mishap, and we all wish we didn't do some things in life. But the thing is that we all need to learn from mistakes and turn them into success, cause only then you will see the true value of failing.

A confident individual looks past failures in his life. Failure is just and parcel of becoming successful. If you failed once, you should make that failure a lesson to learn from.

You have had experiences, and these experiences have produced certain states of consciousness, certain patterns of thought and feeling. You believe certain things about yourself. You act in a certain way because of what you believe. Perhaps it hasn't occurred to you completely, as it probably hasn't to any of us, which you have the authority to forgive or give yourself a new state of consciousness, a new way of life. But you have been given this authority; you have the power to wield it; you can change your outlook on life. Forgiveness is one of the greatest powers we can exercise because it is the activity of infinite love within us.

- **<u>Don't Be Too Hard on Yourself Quotes</u>**

"Gaze up at the star and not at the ground. Try to make sense of what you face in life since every event leads to a wonderful place called experience."-Howard Strachan

"Be true to the game of life, because life will be real to you. If you try to shortcut the game of life, then life will shortcut you. Success doesn't come overnight, so take the time to relax when you get the chance to."-Howard Strachan

"Self-control is the pathway that leads to achieving great things. Nothing can be done without focusing on what you want." Howard Strachan

Live to Win

It doesn't come, in big packages, it is, that small little steps, those small little things. Life is rough, life is tough. Life is complex but becomes simple when you don't compete. Own a style, apply it and see what happens in the end. Devotion will bring you success, don't hide your potential for fear of failure; please let's fly, and on wings as an eagle your spirit, and confidence will forever soar high. Be ready to take corrections though; it's sure worth the try because success comes when you endure.

- **<u>Live to Win Quotes</u>**

"Don't wait for others to appreciate you, it begins with you." –Howard Strachan

"The Journey makes you, while success displays you." –Howard Strachan

"Trust your struggles endure the pain and love your growth." –Howard Strachan

"Life isn't all about what you received or give, but how meek you are when doing it."
–Howard Strachan

Greatness in you

What about you that you furnish that will make you stand out from the competition? Think about yourself, count on your goals, and assume about your dreams. Being in an extraordinary location would not make you great. It's one aspect to have great parents, however, that does not make you great. It's one issue to work for a top-notch company, it's great, however, that doesn't make you brilliant. That wonderful employer or that excellent household that your member of, you are each adding to the greatness of that household or you're diminishing it and it has been noted that it is viable to be in a top-notch house, but you are no longer amazing because you couldn't even be silver you no longer be brass you genuinely be sort or clay a lot of human beings consider that wealth makes you great, however, it is a lot of prosperous people. Who are no longer mind-blowing people, on the one-of-a-kind hand, poverty is equated with greatness in a lot of human beings that if they have nothing they ought to be great. Your greatness is no longer notably primarily based on your income. Some human beings are right at doing, however they're now not right at being.

Greatness will charge you something! It's the price of something that is going to fee you for being different. It is going to feed you some energy, it is going to charge you some hours of your way of life, laying down paying the fee, going the extra mile doing what one-of-a-kind human beings are not inclined to do, greatness is no longer cheap. Greatness is commonly expenditure greater; it is virtually why there are now not many people who gain greatness. They're no longer inclined to pay the price. Greatness is not immediate, in other words, greatness takes time to develop. You cannot truly run into your room and come out great. You do not immediately acquire greatness to continue to be with it. You must acquire skills to continue to be good at it, you've got to retain working only to furnish up too quickly. Greatness will no longer be common, greatness does not longer need the approval of neither man nor woman and if you are that shape of man or woman you will pick out the approval of all humans and the grasp of everyone.

You'll in no way gather greatness, greatness is exceptional you cannot have the approval of each and every individual and be great, and the quicker you apprehend that the faster you do superb in life. You're usually going to stay your existence at the lowest regular denominator of your buddies if you do no longer like it. You cannot be given it as true one way and proceed to be another way and be great.

Greatness is dwelling on what you think about and living up to your full potential usually, you will no longer discover greatness in an individual until they go through hardship. The crisis that brings greatness out of people. There may be something inside an internal reservoir that might no longer lie down and stay down and whine and identify their most three defeated buddies and have a port party, however, there is something about a man or girl that when the waters get and all hell's breaking loose. Greatness will step up to the plate. Sometimes that respects you that in 10 years Or you can pay attention to that advice and it can catapult you to a location of grace, however you have to be teachable to be extremely good you through no means come to a location that you provide up from getting to be aware of gorgeous human beings in no way give up learning human beings who are very professional at what they do nonetheless prefer to analyze how do I get better? How do I get higher at the characteristics of greatness? Is it constantly looking to get higher looking to research more? To be pinnacle notch you have to be in a function to acquire correction, you have to be in a position to be informed you're no longer doing this right

and you have to be capable to being informed with the right attitude.

- ## <u>Greatness in your Quotes</u>

"Inspiration comes from within yourself. One has to be positive, when you're positive, good things take place in your life."-Howard Strachan

"The greatness of a man is not how much he earns but in his integrity and his ability to affect those around him positively."-Howard Strachan

"Never have you procrastinated the power of dreams and the influence of the human spirit. They are the same, greatness lives within each one of us."-Howard Strachan

Be the Best Version of Yourself

I would burn water and freeze fire if you asked; for everywhere you touch a revolution follows, which turns dreams into expeditions. You have a vision, I see your courage. Promise to be legendary and dream in motion. Deep inside you're not the one you wished to be, you're worse than the average, better than what you expect; what are they going to do with you? You're the one they need the most.

- **<u>Be the Best Version of Yourself Quotes</u>**

"What if you're best could be better then your success will be greater."
–Howard Strachan

"Don't be like moon that depends on the sun for light. Instead, be like the stars that have their own source of light."-Howard Strachan

"Like the river and sea, it's the same path we have to take. In order to be where we need to be in life, we first have to settle our differences and move forward." –Howard Strachan

"Success is built on dreams not hope." –Howard Strachan

EXPECT THE BEST

Your attitude toward life determines life's attitude toward you. How you think affects your approach to the successful journey in a powerful way.

What I believe about life determines

How I perceive life, which determines

What I receive from life.

If you expect the worse, you will certainly get it. If you expect the best, even when negative situations comes your way and it seems like there is no way out you can make the best of it and keep going. As long as if you communicate with people in the top organizations across the

country, the higher you go, the better the demeanour you'll discover. A

fortune 700 study found that 94 percent of all the executives surveyed

attributed their success more to attitude than any other factor. That just

goes to show you that if you want to surpass the limit, you must have a

good attitude.

- ### <u>Expect the Best Quotes</u>

"It is easy to hate and it is hard to love. This is how the whole world works. Frankly, all good things are difficult to achieve, and the bad thing is easily gained." -Howard Strachan

"The best preparation for the future is doing what is expected of you today."
-Howard Strachan

"The cost of success is hard work, dedication to the job at hand, and determination which determines whether we will win or fail, so we have to apply the best of ourselves to the task at hand."-Howard Strachan

SUMMING IT UP

The quality of your life is determined by the purposes to which you dedicate yourself. If in these pages you have found ideas that help strengthen and deepen your understanding of the knowledge that requires for success, my purpose is fulfilled. If in the process of sharing insights, we have become friends, I am delighted.
Someone has observed that "once an idea stretches your mind, it will never return to the original length." I pray that you have found in this book ideas that expand your mind and widen your firm of mind about life. It's great to be alive and to be able to learn, work, succeed, and grow into the wonderful person that God said are you to be.

Create the Habit for success

It is important to create the lifestyle that we would like to live, but first, we have to change our bad habits and replace them with successful contributing habits. Time spend confabulate with the wrong people gives you unhappy life, while time spent with people with a success-driven mindset leads to a wealthy life. The thing most people do is that they're playing the universe's most unrewarding game and the game is called follows the blind follower. There is a story about a small town in which there was a bakery store and this store had a clock over the door. Every morning she'd notice a working man stop to adjust his watch the same as the clock timer at the door. He has

been doing this for a few months, one day the baker was returning

back to her store and saw the man, and said "do tell me, why do you

adjust your watch at my door every morning?" the man said, "well,

I'm a foreman for the plant and I want to make sure my watch is

correct because I blow the quitting bell every night at 6 o'clock." The

baker gazed at him and said, that's funny, and I've been setting my

timer at door by that quitting bell all these months. A very logical

thing, but could've been off a few weeks. It was a case of a person just

going along with what he thought was correct without double-

checking her reference. What I would suggest is that from now out

until we do that, we will not know if the person we are following is

leading us in the direction we wish to arrive.

Project to complete

project

deadline

completed

items required

tasks to-do

project

deadline

completed

items required

tasks to-do

Project to complete

project

deadline

completed ☐

items required

tasks to-do

project

deadline

completed ☐

items required

tasks to-do

Project to complete

project	
deadline	completed ☐

items required   **tasks to-do**

☐
☐
☐
☐
☐
☐

project	
deadline	completed ☐

items required   **tasks to-do**

☐
☐
☐
☐
☐
☐

Project to complete

project
deadline
completed

items required
tasks to-do

project
deadline
completed

items required
tasks to-do

Project to complete

project
deadline
completed ☐

items required

tasks to-do

project
deadline
completed ☐

items required

tasks to-do

Project to complete

project
deadline
completed

items required

tasks to-do

project
deadline
completed

items required

tasks to-do

Project to complete

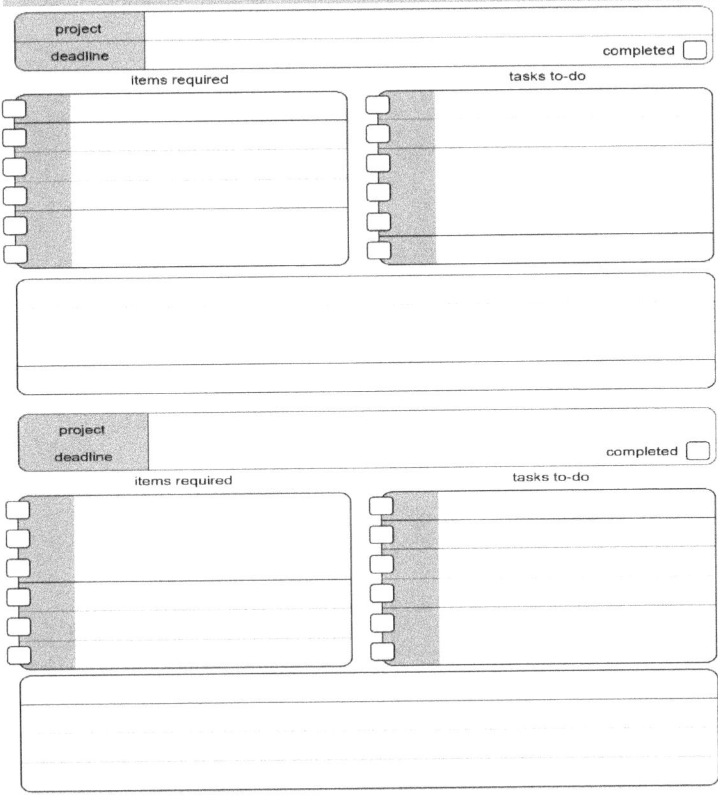

Project to complete

project

deadline

completed ☐

items required

tasks to-do

project

deadline

completed ☐

items required

tasks to-do

Project to complete

project

deadline

completed

items required

tasks to-do

project

deadline

completed

items required

tasks to-do

Project to complete

project
deadline
completed

items required | tasks to-do

project
deadline
completed

items required | tasks to-do

Project to complete

project	
deadline	completed ☐

items required · tasks to-do

project	
deadline	completed ☐

items required · tasks to-do

Project to complete

project

deadline

completed ☐

items required

tasks to-do

---

project

deadline

completed ☐

items required

tasks to-do

Project to complete

<table>
<tr><td>project</td><td></td></tr>
<tr><td>deadline</td><td>completed ☐</td></tr>
</table>

items required

tasks to-do

<table>
<tr><td>project</td><td></td></tr>
<tr><td>deadline</td><td>completed ☐</td></tr>
</table>

items required

tasks to-do

Project to complete

project
deadline
completed ☐

items required

tasks to-do

project
deadline
completed ☐

items required

tasks to-do

Project to complete

project

deadline

completed

items required

tasks to-do

project

deadline

completed

items required

tasks to-do

Habit Tracker

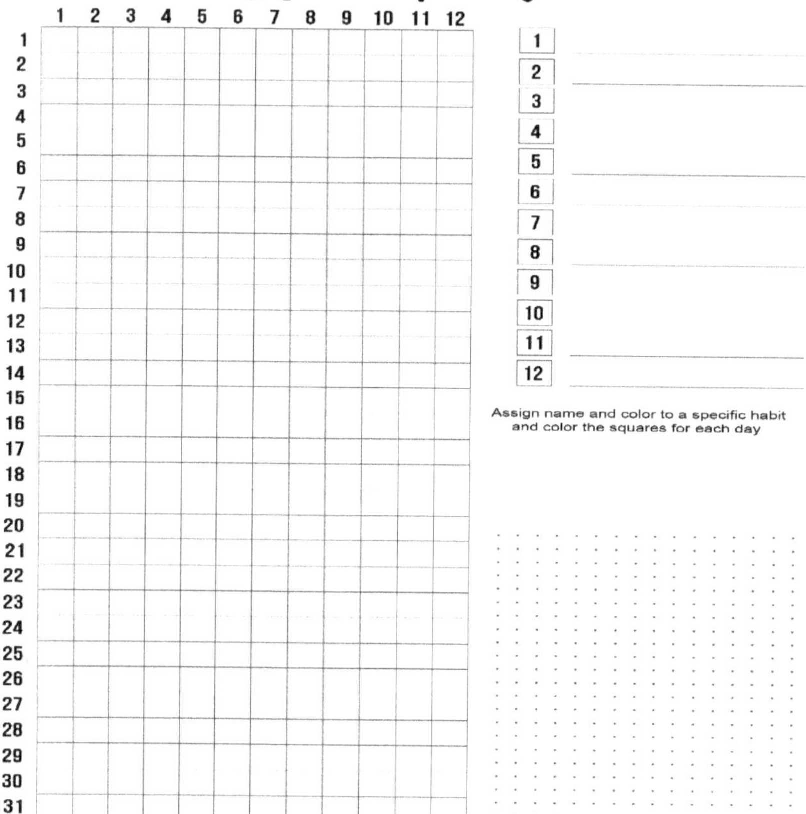

Assign name and color to a specific habit
and color the squares for each day

Habit Tracker

	1	2	3	4	5	6	7	8	9	10	11	12
1												
2												
3												
4												
5												
6												
7												
8												
9												
10												
11												
12												
13												
14												
15												
16												
17												
18												
19												
20												
21												
22												
23												
24												
25												
26												
27												
28												
29												
30												
31												

1
2
3
4
5
6
7
8
9
10
11
12

Assign name and color to a specific habit
and color the squares for each day

Habit Tracker

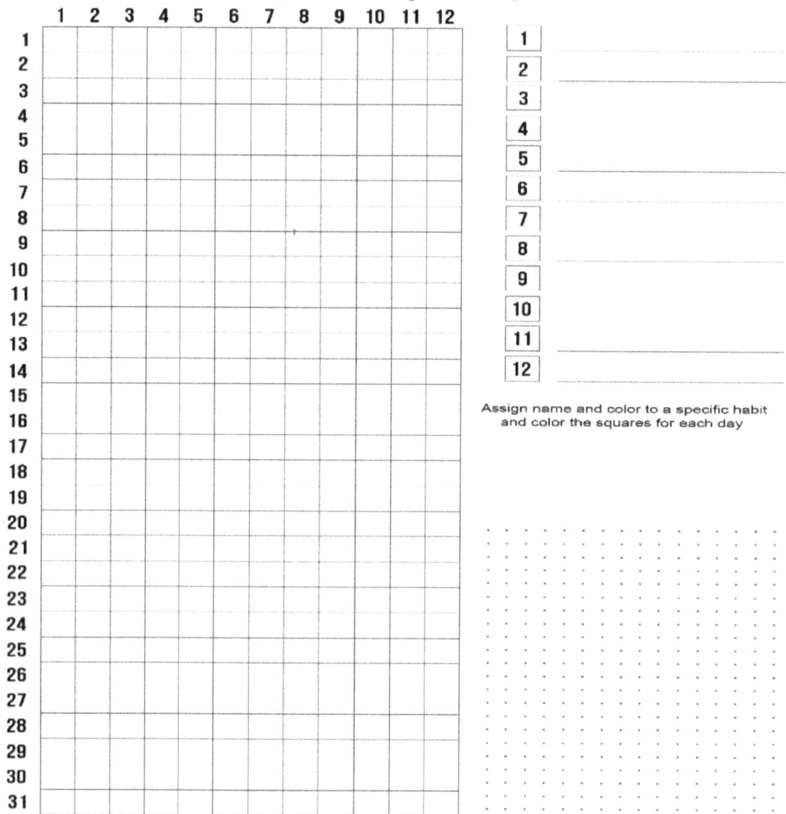

Assign name and color to a specific habit
and color the squares for each day

Habit Tracker

	1	2	3	4	5	6	7	8	9	10	11	12
1												
2												
3												
4												
5												
6												
7												
8												
9												
10												
11												
12												
13												
14												
15												
16												
17												
18												
19												
20												
21												
22												
23												
24												
25												
26												
27												
28												
29												
30												
31												

1	
2	
3	
4	
5	
6	
7	
8	
9	
10	
11	
12	

Assign name and color to a specific habit
and color the squares for each day

Habit Tracker

Assign name and color to a specific habit
and color the squares for each day

Habit Tracker

	1	2	3	4	5	6	7	8	9	10	11	12

1
2
3
4
5
6
7
8
9
10
11
12

Assign name and color to a specific habit
and color the squares for each day

Habit Tracker

| | 1 | 2 | 3 | 4 | 5 | 6 | 7 | 8 | 9 | 10 | 11 | 12 |

1
2
3
4
5
6
7
8
9
10
11
12

Assign name and color to a specific habit
and color the squares for each day

Habit Tracker

	1	2	3	4	5	6	7	8	9	10	11	12
1												
2												
3												
4												
5												
6												
7												
8												
9												
10												
11												
12												
13												
14												
15												
16												
17												
18												
19												
20												
21												
22												
23												
24												
25												
26												
27												
28												
29												
30												
31												

1
2
3
4
5
6
7
8
9
10
11
12

Assign name and color to a specific habit
and color the squares for each day

72

Habit Tracker

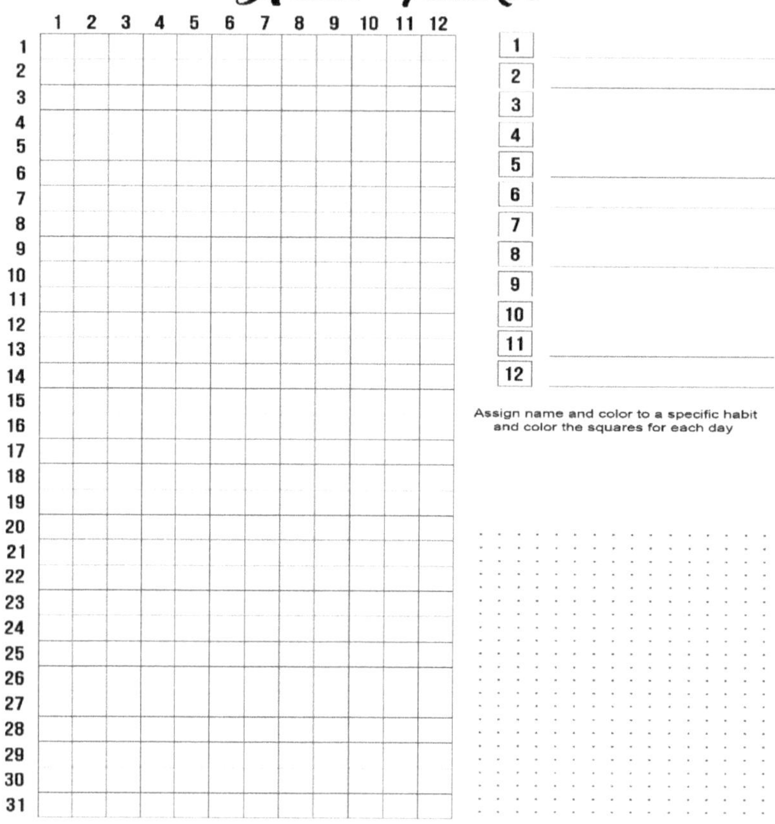

Habit Tracker

Assign name and color to a specific habit
and color the squares for each day

Habit Tracker

	1	2	3	4	5	6	7	8	9	10	11	12
1												
2												
3												
4												
5												
6												
7												
8												
9												
10												
11												
12												
13												
14												
15												
16												
17												
18												
19												
20												
21												
22												
23												
24												
25												
26												
27												
28												
29												
30												
31												

1
2
3
4
5
6
7
8
9
10
11
12

Assign name and color to a specific habit
and color the squares for each day

Habit Tracker

	1	2	3	4	5	6	7	8	9	10	11	12
1												
2												
3												
4												
5												
6												
7												
8												
9												
10												
11												
12												
13												
14												
15												
16												
17												
18												
19												
20												
21												
22												
23												
24												
25												
26												
27												
28												
29												
30												
31												

1. ______
2. ______
3. ______
4. ______
5. ______
6. ______
7. ______
8. ______
9. ______
10. ______
11. ______
12. ______

Assign name and color to a specific habit
and color the squares for each day

Habit Tracker

Assign name and color to a specific habit
and color the squares for each day

Habit Tracker

	1	2	3	4	5	6	7	8	9	10	11	12
1												
2												
3												
4												
5												
6												
7												
8												
9												
10												
11												
12												
13												
14												
15												
16												
17												
18												
19												
20												
21												
22												
23												
24												
25												
26												
27												
28												
29												
30												
31												

1
2
3
4
5
6
7
8
9
10
11
12

Assign name and color to a specific habit
and color the squares for each day

Habit Tracker

	1	2	3	4	5	6	7	8	9	10	11	12
1												
2												
3												
4												
5												
6												
7												
8												
9												
10												
11												
12												
13												
14												
15												
16												
17												
18												
19												
20												
21												
22												
23												
24												
25												
26												
27												
28												
29												
30												
31												

1
2
3
4
5
6
7
8
9
10
11
12

Assign name and color to a specific habit
and color the squares for each day

Habit Tracker

Assign name and color to a specific habit
and color the squares for each day

Habit Tracker

	1	2	3	4	5	6	7	8	9	10	11	12
1												
2												
3												
4												
5												
6												
7												
8												
9												
10												
11												
12												
13												
14												
15												
16												
17												
18												
19												
20												
21												
22												
23												
24												
25												
26												
27												
28												
29												
30												
31												

1
2
3
4
5
6
7
8
9
10
11
12

Assign name and color to a specific habit
and color the squares for each day

Habit Tracker

	1	2	3	4	5	6	7	8	9	10	11	12
1												
2												
3												
4												
5												
6												
7												
8												
9												
10												
11												
12												
13												
14												
15												
16												
17												
18												
19												
20												
21												
22												
23												
24												
25												
26												
27												
28												
29												
30												
31												

1
2
3
4
5
6
7
8
9
10
11
12

Assign name and color to a specific habit
and color the squares for each day

Habit Tracker

	1	2	3	4	5	6	7	8	9	10	11	12
1												
2												
3												
4												
5												
6												
7												
8												
9												
10												
11												
12												
13												
14												
15												
16												
17												
18												
19												
20												
21												
22												
23												
24												
25												
26												
27												
28												
29												
30												
31												

1
2
3
4
5
6
7
8
9
10
11
12

Assign name and color to a specific habit
and color the squares for each day

Habit Tracker

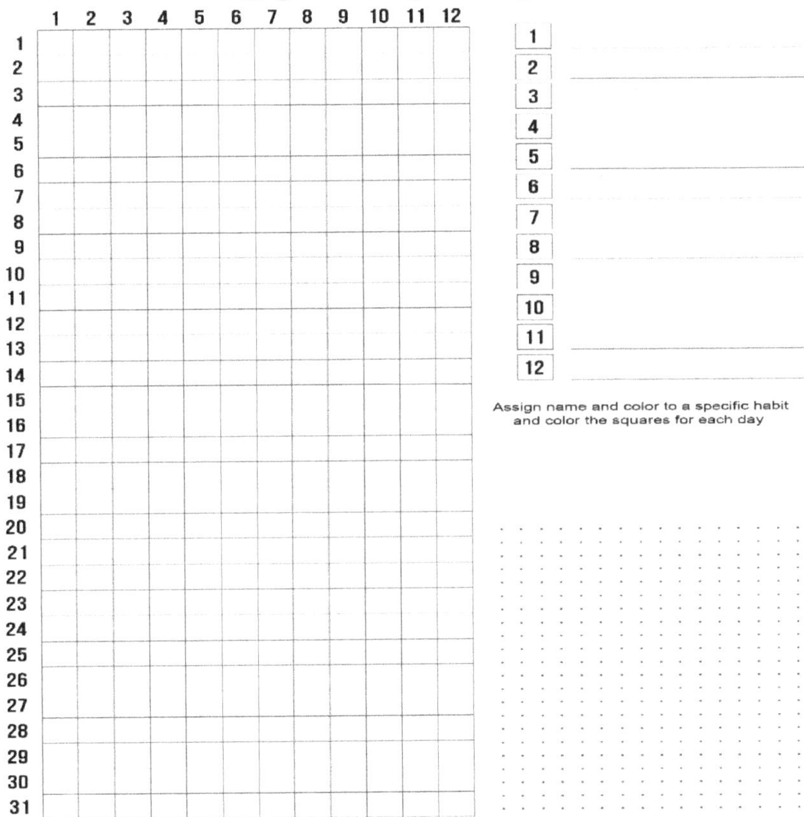

Assign name and color to a specific habit
and color the squares for each day

Habit Tracker

Assign name and color to a specific habit
and color the squares for each day